First World War
and Army of Occupation
War Diary
France, Belgium and Germany

28 DIVISION
Divisional Troops
Divisional Ammunition Column
29 December 1914 - 31 October 1915

WO95/2271/7

The Naval & Military Press Ltd
www.nmarchive.com
Published in association with The National Archives

Published by

The Naval & Military Press Ltd

Unit 10 Ridgewood Industrial Park,

Uckfield, East Sussex,

TN22 5QE England

Tel: +44 (0) 1825 749494

www.naval-military-press.com

www.nmarchive.com

This diary has been reprinted in facsimile from the original. Any imperfections are inevitably reproduced and the quality may fall short of modern type and cartographic standards.

© Crown Copyright
Images reproduced by permission of The National Archives, London, England, 2015.

Contents

Document type	Place/Title	Date From	Date To
Heading	WO95/2271-7		
Heading	28th Divl Ammn Column Dec 1914-Oct 1915		
Heading	28th Divl Ammn Coln Vol I 29.12.14-31.1.15		
Heading	War Diary Of 28th Divisional Ammn Column from 29th Dec 1914 to 31st January 1915		
War Diary	Slough	29/12/1914	17/01/1915
War Diary	Southampton	17/01/1915	17/01/1915
War Diary	Harve	18/01/1915	28/01/1915
Heading	28th Divl Ammn Coln Vol I 1-28.2.15		
War Diary	Borre	07/02/1915	28/02/1915
Heading	28th Divl Ammn Coln Vol III 1-31.2.15		
War Diary	Poperinghe	01/03/1915	25/03/1915
Heading	28th Divl Ammn Coln. Vol IV		
Heading	War Diary 28th Divisional Ammunition Column April 1915		
War Diary	Poperinghe	05/04/1915	30/04/1915
Heading	War Diary 28th Divisional Ammunition Column May 1915		
War Diary	Poperinghe	01/05/1915	03/05/1915
War Diary	Abeele	05/05/1915	31/05/1915
Heading	War Diary 28th Divisional Ammunition Column June 1915		
War Diary	Winnezeele	01/06/1915	18/06/1915
War Diary	Westoutre	21/06/1915	27/06/1915
Heading	28th Divl. Ammn Coln Vol V 3-13-7-15		
Heading	War Diary 28th Divisional Ammunition Column July 1915		
War Diary	Westoutre	01/07/1915	09/07/1915
War Diary	Berthen	13/07/1915	13/07/1915
Heading	28th Divl. Ammn Coln Vol VI From 8th To 19th August 1915		
War Diary	Berthen	08/08/1915	19/08/1915
Heading	28th Divl Ammn Coln Vol VII Sept 15		
War Diary	Berthen	04/09/1915	23/09/1915
War Diary	Borre	24/09/1915	26/09/1915
War Diary	Quentin	26/09/1915	27/09/1915
War Diary	Fouquereuil	27/04/1915	29/04/1915
War Diary	Vendin	29/04/1915	29/04/1915
Heading	28th Divl Ammn Col. Oct 15 Vol VIII		
Heading	War Diary 28th Div. Amm Col October		
War Diary	Vendin	01/10/1915	20/10/1915
War Diary	Fouquereuil	23/10/1915	23/10/1915
War Diary	Marseilles	25/10/1915	31/10/1915

W095/22711

28TH DIVISION
DIVL ARTILLERY

28TH DIVL AMN COLUMN
DEC 1914 - OCT 1915

28TH DIVISION
DIVL ARTILLERY

121/4327

S.S. "Rio Claro" & Co.

Vol I. 29.12.14 — 31.1.15

Confidential

War Diary
of
28th Divisional Ammn Column

from 29th Decr 1914 to 31st January 1915

Army Form C. 2118.

WAR DIARY
or
INTELLIGENCE SUMMARY
(Erase heading not required.)

281st DAC

Instructions regarding War Diaries and Intelligence Summaries are contained in F. S. Regs., Part II. and the Staff Manual respectively. Title pages will be prepared in manuscript.

Hour, Date, Place	Summary of Events and Information	Remarks and references to Appendices
29th Dec 1914 at SLOUGH	Unit mobilized - The personnel was drawn chiefly from Territorials. The WESSEX HANTS RGA & DEVON RFA being completed by regulars from the 1st Reserve Bde RFA at NEWCASTLE	JA
1st Jan 15 at SLOUGH	Sections & Head Quarters were organised & Officers allotted.	JA
2nd Jan to 16th Jan 1915 SLOUGH	Receiving Stores, issuing same to sections. Receiving horses, spotting harness. Loading ammunition wagons	JA
17th Jan 1915, SLOUGH	The Column entrained for SOUTHAMPTON in two trains, the first leaving at 6.30 AM & the last at 1.15 PM. Considering the untrained condition of the majority of the men and the horses the entraining must be considered very successfully performed	JA
17th Jan 1915 SOUTHAMPTON 6.30 PM.	Embarked at SOUTHAMPTON and left at	JA
18th Jan 1915, HAVRE 8 AM	Arrived off pier and had hard a considerable time before entering the docks to disembark	JA
11 AM	Entered the docks and commenced disembarkation which was completed by about 6 PM	JA
18 Jan 1915 HAVRE 10 PM	Left the Column & left for N° 2 Rest Camp Distance from the docks to Camp about 7 miles	JA

1247 W 3229 200,000 (E) 8/14 J.B.C. & A. Forms/C. 2118/11.

Army Form C. 2118.

WAR DIARY
or
INTELLIGENCE SUMMARY

(Erase heading not required.)

28 DAC

Hour, Date, Place	Summary of Events and Information	Remarks and references to Appendices
21st Jan/15 4.30AM 9 AM 11.30 AM 2 PM	No 1 Section entrained No 3 Section entrained " 2 Section entrained " 4 Section entrained	JM
22nd Jan/15	Detrained at HAZEBROUCK and proceeded to Billets south of BORRE	JM
28th Jan 1915 2pm	Inspection by Field Marshal Sir JOHN FRENCH at PRADELLES. Drew marching order, dismounted	JM

Instructions regarding War Diaries and Intelligence Summaries are contained in F.S. Regs., Part II. and the Staff Manual respectively. Title pages will be prepared in manuscript.

1247 W 3299 200,000 (E) 8/11 J.B.C. & A.   Forms/C. 2118/11.

28th Div d'Armée Col
Vol II 1 - 28.2.15

Army Form C. 2118.

WAR DIARY
or
INTELLIGENCE SUMMARY
(Erase heading not required.)

28th Divisional Am. Column

Instructions regarding War Diaries and Intelligence Summaries are contained in F. S. Regs, Part II. and the Staff Manual respectively. Title pages will be prepared in manuscript.

Hour, Date, Place	Summary of Events and Information	Remarks and references to Appendices
7am 7th February 1915 BORRE	Left BORRE and proceeded by march route to POPERINGHE via CAESTRE and STEENVOORDE. POPERINGHE reached by 1pm. The march was well carried out and no casualties occurred. Went into billets in an area East-South East of POPERINGHE	JTA
15th February 1915	No 1 Section supplied the 3rd Brigade RFA Ammunition Column with 840 rds of 18th Shrapnel, at the refilling point ½ mile south of VLAMERTINGHE. — This was the first supply of Ammunition made by the Column	JTA
28th February 1915	The Column moved into a new billeting area — North of the POPERINGHE — ABEELE Rd.	JTA

28ter Diol: Comm. "Cob."

Vol III 1 – 31.3.45

Army Form C. 2118.

WAR DIARY
or
INTELLIGENCE SUMMARY

(Erase heading not required.)

28th Divisional Amm'n Column

March 1915

Hour, Date, Place	Summary of Events and Information	Remarks and references to Appendices
1st March POPERINGHE	Establishment increased by 4 GS wagons for 4.5" How'r Amn. These were received from 5th DAC	JTA
9th March POPERINGHE	Establishment reduced by 12 GS wagons. These were sent from No 4 Section to the following:- 4 to No 115 Heavy Am'n Column 4 " " 116 " " " 4 " " 121 " " " On the same date the establishment was increased by 198 wagons to carry explosives.	JTA JTA
25th March POPERINGHE 4.30 P.M.	The Column was inspected by Lt Genl Plumer Com'dg 5th Army Corps.	JTA

W. Kennich

S.Colerta
Com dg 28 DAC

28th Division

D/6344

28th Div: Ammⁿ Colⁿ
Vol IV
5-4-27-6-15

War Diary

28th Divisional Ammunition Column

April 1915

Confidential

Army Form C. 2118.

WAR DIARY
or
INTELLIGENCE SUMMARY
(Erase heading not required.)

Instructions regarding War Diaries and Intelligence Summaries are contained in F. S. Regs, Part II. and the Staff Manual respectively. Title pages will be prepared in manuscript.

Hour, Date, Place	Summary of Events and Information	Remarks and references to Appendices
Apl. 5th POPERINGHE	G.S. Wagon received from 27th Divisional Train	M.Y
" 7th do.	do do 5th Northumberland Fusiliers	M.Y
" 13' do.	do. do. 27th Divisional Train	M.Y
" 18' do.	No. III* Section moved as "advanced section" to Billets 1 mile east of POPERINGHE Railway Station, close to and South of POPERINGHE — VLAMERTINGHE road.	M.Y
8.20 p.m. 22nd do.	Orders received to "Stand by".	M.Y
	Column stood by, (ready to move) all night.	M.Y
April 19th to 30th do.	All horses kept harnessed up by night and one half day wheelers being hooked in.	M.Y
	Ammunition issued during the month.	
	18 pr.: Shrapnel 23,164 H.E. 1,126	
	4.5" " 965 Lyd. 3,541.	
	S.A.A. 5,731,000.	
	Largest issue within 24 hours was for 24th — 25th viz:—	
	18 pr. Shrapnel 3,864, S.A.A 477,000, 4.5" Shrapnel 286	M.Y

W. Ulrich Lt. Col
Comdg. 28th Bird. Amm. Col.

War Diary.

28th Divisional Ammunition Column.

May 1915

Confidential

Army Form C. 2118.

WAR DIARY
or
INTELLIGENCE SUMMARY
(Erase heading not required.)

Instructions regarding War Diaries and Intelligence Summaries are contained in F.S. Regs., Part II. and the Staff Manual respectively. Title pages will be prepared in manuscript.

Hour, Date, Place		Summary of Events and Information	Remarks and references to Appendices
May 1st to 3rd	POPERINGHE	Moved to billets close to ABEELE, between ABEELE — POPERINGHE Road and railway.	H.Y
May 5th	ABEELE	Arranged to refill Sections I and III at Section II billets.	H.Y
May 31st	ABEELE	Marched via WATOU to rest-billets close to and East of WINNEZEELE.	H.Y
		Ammunition issued during the month:—	
		18 pr. Shrapnel 44,508 H.E. 488.	
		4.5" do. 3932 Lyd. 4,032	
		S.A.A. 2,989,000	
		During the 24 hours May 8th–9th and May 24th–25th always the Column was Ammunitionnaires fully occupied. Men and horses worked well. Ammunition issued as under	H.Y

	May 8th–9th		May 24th–25th	
Sect I	5258	400,000	2 016	60,000
II	1216	—	5 056	280,000
III	4268	—	3,192	—
Total	10742	400,000	10264	340,000
4.5"	282	1002	344	—
	Shrap. Lyd.	SAA	Shrap. Lyd.	S.A.A.

W. Keswick Lt. Col
Cmdg 28th Div. Amm. Col

War Diary

28th Divisional Ammunition Column

June 1915.

Confidential

WAR DIARY
or
INTELLIGENCE SUMMARY

(Erase heading not required.)

Army Form C. 2118.

Instructions regarding War Diaries and Intelligence Summaries are contained in F. S. Regs., Part II. and the Staff Manual respectively. Title pages will be prepared in manuscript.

Hour, Date, Place	Summary of Events and Information	Remarks and references to Appendices
June 1st WINNEZEELE	Moved about 1½ miles to fresh billets East of WINNEZEELE — STEENWOORDE road.	M
4" do	Moved to billets close to and West of WINNEZEELE.	M
7"	No. IV section moved to VLAMERTINGHE to be attached to VII "D.A.C.	M
18"	Column less No IV section marched via STEENWOORDE — ABEELE — BOESCHEPE to billets west of WESTOUTRE.	M
	The following details were attached from 14th D.A.C. for service of Howitzer Battery of the Division :— 3 Wagons G.S.; 21 L.D. horses and mules; 15 N.C.Os. and men.	
21st WESTOUTRE	Supply of hand- and rifle-grenades taken over by Brit. Amm Col. from R.E.	
	No. IV section now attached to IV" D.A.C.	
	Ammunition issued by sections I, II , III	
	18pr. Shrapnel 1514 ; H.E. 360 — S.A.A. 816,000.	

W. Kurrich 2/Lieut.
Cmdg 28 Bri. Am. Col.

28th Division

121/6344

28th Divl Amn Coln

Vol V

3-1-3-4-15

War Diary.

28th Divisional Ammunition Column

July 1915.

Army Form C. 2118.

WAR DIARY
or
INTELLIGENCE SUMMARY
(Erase heading not required.)

Instructions regarding War Diaries and Intelligence Summaries are contained in F.S. Regs., Part II. and the Staff Manual respectively. Title pages will be prepared in manuscript.

Hour, Date, Place	Summary of Events and Information	Remarks and references to Appendices
July 1st July 3rd WESTOUTRE	D.A.C. changed into supply of 40mm and 4pr Trench How. gn Ammun. for No IV Section transferred to IV" S.A.C. and establishment accordingly reduced to:- Officers 13. Other ranks 358: Riders 40: H.D.379. G.S. Wagons 83: Watercarts 2. Maltese cart 1. Bicycles 5. plus attached from Divisional Train, 7 G.S. wagons, 7 drivers, 14 H.D. horses.	N.V.
6" – 7" do	A party of 1 Officer and 100 men dug in R.A. telephone wires near DICKE BUSCH ※	N.V.
9" do	Details previously attached from 14" D.H.C. now posted. Establishment increased to: Officers 13. Other ranks 374. Riders 41. H.D. 379. 22. or Mules 20. G.S. Wagons 86: Watercarts 2. Maltese cart 1. Bicycles 5 plus attached from Divisional Train, 7 G.S. wagons, 7 drivers, 14 H.D. horses.	N.V.
13" BERTHEN	Marched (about 2 miles) to fresh billets close to and south of BERTHEN – H.Q. and Sect III were billeted in farms on the BERTHEN – ST JANS CAPPEL road; Sects I, II in farms a short distance west of it.	N.V.
	※ Digging parties, average strength 1 Officer and 50 men, have been used almost every night during the month.	N.V.
13"	510,000 Rds. S.A.A. returned to Park to reduce supplies in first of railhead. Ammunition issued during month. 18pr Shrapnel 4128 rds, H.E. 440. +5" Shrapnel 366 do; Lyd. 294 rds – S.A.A. 741,000 rds. 4pr Trench Howitzer 1,000 Rds. 40mm Trench Howitzer 90 di weary. 95 H.E shr.	N.V. W.Kenrick Lt Col. Cmdg 28" Div Amm Col

1247 W 3299 200,000 (E) 8/14 J.B.C. & A. Forms/C. 2118/11.

28th Division.

12/6529

28th Divl: Annex "C" &c
Vol VI
From 8th to 19th August 1915

Army Form C. 2118.

WAR DIARY
or
INTELLIGENCE SUMMARY
(Erase heading not required.)

Instructions regarding War Diaries and Intelligence Summaries are contained in F. S. Regs., Part II. and the Staff Manual respectively. Title pages will be prepared in manuscript.

Hour, Date, Place	Summary of Events and Information	Remarks and references to Appendices
Aug. 8th BERTHEN	D.A.C. details for 2 Howitzer 4.5" batteries (each 3 wagons and personnel) posted to B.A.C.. Details from A/73 posted to Section I, B/89 to Section II, A/49 (which joined BAC in June) to Sect III. Each section now has B.A.C. details for the Howitzer battery which is incorporated in the R F A Bde. it supplies. Establishment to be increased: extent under consideration.	HV
	183	
Aug. 10th BERTHEN	Not posted. L.D. horses received, and 113 H.D released. 32 Sections developed for 60 extra horses	HV
	Digging party by night, cancelled: works by day instead.	HV
Aug. 17th do.	Digging party increased to 1 officer and 80 O.R.	HV
Aug. 16 do.	All 18 pr. H.E. returned to railhead. Authy QMG 9/82 SQR96d-13:8.15 HV and replaced by shrapnel. Second batch of 183 L.D animals (mules) received, and 100 H.D released.	HV
Aug. 19th do	32 extra drivers received.	HV
	Ammunition issued during the month:	
	18 pr. Shrapnel 4924 rds. H.E. 312	
	4.5" Howitzer. Shrapnel 614 Lyd. 338	
	S.A.A. 990,000.	
		HV Wr Minich Lt.Col. RFA
		Comdg. 28th Divl. Amm. Col.

1247 W 3259 200,000 (E) 8/14 J.B.C. & A. Forms/C. 2118/11.

121/7107

38th Division

28th Div: Amm "Col"
Vol VII
Sep 15

WAR DIARY or INTELLIGENCE SUMMARY

(Erase heading not required.)

Army Form C. 2118.

Hour, Date, Place	Summary of Events and Information	Remarks and references to Appendices
September 4th BERTHEN	Column reorganized on the lines of War Estb. Part VII (New armies) 1915 — The Howitzer section is abolished; number of wagons for 18 pr. ammunition is reduced by 1 to 56; and 8 wagons for 4·5" ammunition are added. 9 are left, pending decision on future raised — D.A.C. now has 88 wagons for ammunition and carries 600 6068 rds. 18 pr. — 528 rds. 4·5" — 930,000 rds. S.A.A. Establishment consists of 11 Officers and Medical Officer, 4 Warrant Officers, 514 other ranks and 7 attached including Train; horses (including attached and excluding Train) 50 Riders or Chargers, 605 L.D. (horses + mules)	A.G. G.H.Q. D/123. H.V.
September 12th BERTHEN	Part Estb. of L.D. horses arrived and all H.D. returned.	H.V.
21st do.	Establishment of S.A.A. reduced to 929,000.	H.V.
22nd do.	Manned No. I section Canadian D.A.C. arrived, preparatory to Canadian D.A.C. taking over from 28th D.A.C.	H.V.
10 am do.	Section III left for BORRE by road. Remainder of Canadian D.A.C. arrived and took over from 28th D.A.C.	H.V.
23rd do.	28th D.A.C. less section III moved by road to BORRE (8 miles) leaving at 9 am. — In billets by 2 pm.	H.V.

Page 2.

Army Form C. 2118.

WAR DIARY
or
INTELLIGENCE SUMMARY
(Erase heading not required.)

Instructions regarding War Diaries and Intelligence Summaries are contained in F. S. Regs., Part II. and the Staff Manual respectively. Title pages will be prepared in manuscript.

Hour, Date, Place		Summary of Events and Information	Remarks and references to Appendices
24 September	BORRE	Found extra S.A.A. to infantry (50 rds. per man) to be carried by infantry in case of move by motor-bus, or to be collected by D.A.C. if move by road instead.	H.H.
26 September	BORRE	Collected extra S.A.A. from infantry on move by road being ordered. 116,000 rounds deficient. Left BORRE at 2 p.m. for billets in area M and N. of LE PARADIS, South of MERVILLE. Road blocked by traffic. Area found to be occupied by 34th Infy. Bde., so proceeded to QUENTIN where settled in billets by 8 p.m.	H.H.
10 p.m. 26 September	QUENTIN	Filled up S.A.A. from Park. Emake up deficiency.	H.H
2 p.m. 27"	"	Left for FOUQUEREUIL, 7 miles.	
8 p.m. 27"	FOUQUEREUIL	In billets by 8 p.m.	H.H.
2 p.m. 29"	"	Left by road, 3 miles march for VENDIN.	
5 p.m. 29"	VENDIN	In billets.	
8.10 p.m. 29"	"	28th Inf. Park "departed" at VENDIN - 3600 rds. 18 pr. shrapnel, 960,000 S.A.A., 480 rds. 4.5" Hyd., Ammunition Lorries Composition	

18 pr - shrapnel 2,952	- H.E. 108	
4.5" hydrate 568	- shrapnel 208	
1.5" Trench Mortar 60	S.A.A. 1,884,000	
4 pr. Nil		

W. Kenrick
Andy 28th D.A.C.

1247 W 3299 200,000 (E) 8/14 J.B.C. & A. Forms/C. 2118/11.

121/7466

38th Known

28th Div. Armr. Cal.

Oct -15

Vol XII VIII

M

WAR DIARY
28th DIV. AMM. COL.
OCTOBER

WAR DIARY or **INTELLIGENCE SUMMARY**

(Erase heading not required.)

Army Form C. 2118.

Hour, Date, Place		Summary of Events and Information	Issues 18 /pr 4.5"						Remarks and references to Appendices
			Shrap	H.E.	Total	Lyd	Lachri mats	Total	SAA Thousands
October 1st to 4th	VENDIN	Ammu. issued as under →	17308	4448	21456	1586	266	1832	139	H.Y.
October 10th	–11th	do.	2912	3272	6184	484	134	618	
" 11	–12	do.	1232	3248	4480	384	256	640	
" 12	–13	do.	3472	4372	7844	1786		1786	
" 13	–14	do.	4532	4740	9272	1474	244	1718	
" 14 –17 (12 noon)	do.	do.	5264	3584	8848	2608		2608	H.Y.
October 20th	VENDIN	D.A.C. moved 7 miles by road to HAUT RIEUX							
October 23rd	FOUQUEREUIL	D.A.C. entrained in 4 trains. H.Q. with sections from I, 5 from II, and 6 from III. Last section due to leave at 12.35 p.m. 6 from III, last section with 23 wagons each, in trains at 3 hours' interval.							H.Y.
October 25th	MARSEILLES	Arrived and proceeded to camp at PARC BORÉLY.							H.Y.
October 29	do.	9 gunners inspected. Mallein test begun.							H.Y.
" 30	do.	4 horses and 1 mule reported sick. Destroyed							H.Y.
" 31	do.	3 do. 2 do do do							

Ammunition issued during the month. 43728 42084 85812 11316 1166 13482 275
W. Kennies Lt. Col. R.A. comdg 28 D.A.C.

www.ingramcontent.com/pod-product-compliance
Lightning Source LLC
Chambersburg PA
CBHW081503160426
43193CB00014B/2579